DISCARDED

DATE DUE

AP 23 79			
MY 8 '79 MAY 30 80			
JAN 7			
JAN 17			
FEB 9			

Great Britain

Managing editor Chris Milsome
Editor Chester Fisher
Assistant Editor Dale Gunthorp
Design Patrick Frean
Picture Research Ed Harriman
Production Phillip Hughes
Illustrations John Shackell
　　　　　　　Ron Hayward
　　　　　　　John Mousdale
　　　　　　　Marilyn Day
　　　　　　　Tony Payne
Maps Matthews and Taylor Associates

Photographic sources: Key to positions
of illustrations: (T) top, (C) centre,
(B) bottom, (L) left, (R) right.
ATV: *29(TL)* Australian Information
Service: *18(BR)* Liz Braddell: *48(B)*
British Hovercraft Corporation: *33(BR)*
British Museum: *42(B)* British Museum
(Natural History): *8(T)* British
Petroleum: *52(TC)* BPC Picture Library:
*12(BC), 22(BC), 24(BL), 28(TL),
35(BR), 39(TL), 51(TR)* British Steel
Corporation: *10(C), 34(T)* British
Tourist Authority: *6-7, 21(BL), 21(TR),
21(BR), 27(BR), 38(CL), 38(BC),
41(BR), 51(BR)* Butlins: *20(B)* Camera
Press: *52(TC), 53(BL)* Central Office of
Information, Crown Copyright: *39(BR)*
Colin Craig: *25(TL)* Colorsport: *18(T),
18(BL)* Mary Evans Picture Library:
*9(BL), 12(TC), 13(TL), 29(TR),
29(CR), 33(TR), 42(BL)* Sonia Halliday
Photographs: *2-3, 8(B), 10(TL), 10(B),
17(BR), 21(BR), 23(BR), 31(TR),
49(TL), 50(BR), 52(BR)* Ed Harriman:
25(TR), 37(BR) Imperial War Museum
London: *45(T)* Dennis Moore: *14-15,
16(TR), 16(B), 17(TC), 22(TC),
23(BL), 24(TL), 25(BR), 27(BL),
29(BL), 30(T), 30(BL), 37(TL),
37(TR), 37(BL), 43(TL), 45(BR),
50(BL), 51(TC), 53(BR)* National Coal
Board: *34(B)* National Gallery London:
30(BC) National Portrait Gallery:
41(BC) Radio Times Hulton Picture
Library: *31(C), 32(CL), 33(CL),
40(T), 40(B), 41(TL), 43(TR), 43(BL),
44(CL), 44(BL), 44(BR), 45(BL)* Royal
Court Theatre: *29(BR)* Syndication
International: *47(B)* Tate Gallery:
31(TL) Tesco Supermarkets: *24(BC)*
United Press International: *53(TR)*
Reg Wilson: *31(BR)*

First published 1975
Macdonald Educational Limited
Holywell House
London, E. C. 2

© Macdonald Educational
Limited 1975

ISBN 0 356 04855 1

Published in the United
States by Silver Burdett
Company, Morristown, N. J.
1976 Printing

Library of Congress
Catalog Card No. 75-44870

Great Britain

the land and its people

Francis Coleman

Macdonald Educational

914.2
Col

6

Contents

254-70

The makings of the British

Invasion and Settlement

Britain was covered with great ice sheets and glaciers until about 7,000 B.C. The few thousand inhabitants of Britain at the end of the last Ice Age, in such places as the Thames Valley, were hunters using stone and bone tools.

When the ice had melted, the sea-level rose and Britain became an island. Settlers from Europe introduced farming, pottery and new implements from about 3,500 B.C. Further settlers brought the knowledge of bronze from about 1,850 B.C.

More settlers from Europe, principally the Celts, introduced iron into Britain about 550 B.C. They established vigorous settlements throughout Britain.

When Julius Caesar invaded Britain in 55 B.C. he was met by strong organized opposition which repulsed his first invasion. It was left to the Emperor Claudius almost a century later to conquer and establish Roman order in Britain. Scotland with its fierce tribes of Picts and Scots remained unconquered.

▲ The oldest human remains found in Britain were at Swanscombe in Kent. This reconstruction of a hunting expedition could have taken place 250,000 years ago.

▼ Stonehenge, built about 2,000 B.C., was the first major British work of architecture. It is thought that it was a temple for the worship of the sun.

The End of Roman Britain

The Romans, despite their civilizing influence were just visitors. They withdrew in the fifth century A.D. and almost at once barbarian tribes of Angles, Saxons and Jutes began to invade Britain. Romanized Britons fought against them but were finally pushed into remoter parts such as Wales, Devon and Cornwall. Britain became an isolated pagan country in which Christianity survived in only a few Celtic outposts.

Another assault on Britain came from Scandinavia, in the form of the fierce Vikings in the ninth century. At first merely raiding and pillaging, they later conquered and began settlements.

The last invasion came in 1066 from France. William the Conqueror claimed the throne and overwhelmed Saxon opposition in 1066. The Normans desired to be overlords of all Britain but Scotland resisted all attempts and Wales did not submit until 1282.

▲ A Saxon. After the Romans had abandoned Britain in the fifth century A.D. Angles and Saxons from Germany conquered and gradually settled in the country.

▲ A Viking. In the eighth century A.D. Vikings arrived from Scandinavia. They came as raiders, but later settled and became farmers.

▲ Julius Caesar invades Britain in 55 B.C. A fierce battle on the beach near Dover was won by Roman discipline and superior weapons. Nearly a century later the Romans colonized Britain, bringing a civilization far in advance of that of the native Briton.

The many invasions of Britain

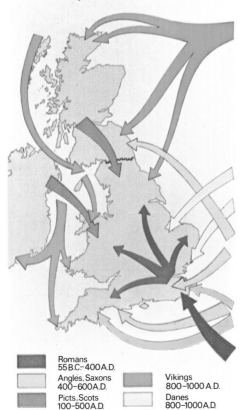

Romans 55 B.C.–400 A.D.	
Angles, Saxons 400–600 A.D.	Vikings 800–1000 A.D.
Picts, Scots 100–500 A.D.	Danes 800–1000 A.D.
Jutes 400 A.D.	Normans 1066 A.D.

▲ A Norman. In 1066 the Normans, under William the Conqueror, invaded England. Norman soldiers who had fought Harold's English army were rewarded with estates.

A compact and fascinating land

Scotland and Wales can boast of ranges of mountains; Scotland also has fiorded coast lines with tumultuous seas and several deep lakes. Yet, on the whole, Britain is made on a small scale, a human scale.

Though urban sprawl disfigures large areas of green fields and woodland, much natural beauty remains. Most visitors are impressed by rural Britain yet most see only a small part. The Forest of Dean, Cumberland's wilder places and the Highlands of Scotland are known to only a few. Famous rural areas, like the Lake District and the coastlines of Devon and Cornwall, become very crowded in the summer, for millions of tourists visit Britain every year. Many tourists are surprised by the smallness of Britain. Yet the island supports a population of more than 54 million people. Despite the pressures of this vast population, there is a strong desire to preserve natural and historical beauty.

▲ The valley of Glencoe in the Scottish highlands—a mountainous, sparsely populated and scenically beautiful region. Scotland has become an important centre for tourism. Scots remember that in this valley, the horrible Glencoe massacre of Highlanders occurred in 1692.

▶ The Welsh valleys have a magical pull, for Wales is the land of druids, and one of the retreats of the ancient British. Industries, particularly coal and steel, have now marked the romantic green valleys.

▼ Old Bosham in Sussex typifies the lure of the rural south of England. The gentle climate and fairytale natural beauty make the south a popular place for retirement and holidays. Many former fishing villages have become places of escape from urban life.

Things to see in Great Britain

SCOTLAND
1 St. Andrew's Cross, Flag of Scotland.
2 Tartan of Macgregor.
3 Tartan of Macleod.
4 Loch Ness, home of the legendary monster, near Inverness.
5 "Bonnie Prince Charlie" (Charles Stuart). 1745-6 tried to assert his right to the British Crown but was defeated at Culloden Moor.
6 Ben Nevis. Highest point in Britain (1,341 m.).
7 Typical Scottish castle. Craisievar Castle, Aberdeen.
8 Oil Rig in North Sea.
9 Modern trawler from Aberdeen.

NORTH ENGLAND
10 Coin showing Britannia issued by the Roman Emperor Hadrian.
11 Hadrian's Wall at Haltcastle.
12 Shipbuilding at Newcastle/Tees.
13 The Venerable Bede, "the father of English history" wrote at Jarrow.
14 Holy Island (Lindisfarne) ancient outpost of Christianity.
15 Longstone Lighthouse and Grace Darling. Grace heroically rescued sailors from a sinking ship in 1838.

EAST ANGLIA
16 Crops of East Anglia.
17 Flat Fenland landscape.
18 Windmills in Suffolk and Norfolk.
19 Reed collecting in Norfolk.
20 Thatch work on Norfolk cottage.

MIDDLE ENGLAND
21 Warwickshire, home of Shakespeare.
22 House of Tudor period, Stratford.
23 Warwickshire landscape.
24 Staffordshire, pottery centre.
25 Concorde, built at Bristol.
26 Oxford University.
27 Great Tom Tower, Oxford.
28 Heavy industry, Birmingham/Coventry.
29 Centre for car-making

WALES
30 Harlech Castle, Merioneth.
31 Mining valleys of Rhondda, Wales
32 National dress of Wales.
33 Lyn Lydaw in Snowdonia.
34 The Welsh dragon. Symbol of Wales.

SOUTHERN ENGLAND
35 Oast houses for drying hops, Kent.
36 Kent, the "Garden of England"
37 Banner of the Cinque Ports.
38 Dover Castle, Kent.
39 Figurehead, Chatham Naval Dockyard.
40 Piers of south coast: Brighton/Margate.
41 White cliffs of Sussex/Kent.

WEST COUNTRY
42 Abandoned 19th century tin mine.
43 Tourist beaches in Cornwall.
44 St. Michael's Mount, Cornwall.
45 The Harbour of Polperro.

The British influence

▶ Britain was the first country to industrialize on a large scale. The "Industrial revolution" during the late 18th and early 19th centuries was largely due to the British genius for invention. Seen here is the steam hammer invented by James Nasmyth in 1842. Larger countries with more resources were soon to challenge Britain's lead in industry.

The legacy of empire

Britain is one of the makers of the mode world. Its great influence came from success in developing a world-wide tradi empire.

The British Empire was the largest t world has ever known. A British impr was left on every country she coloniz English with all its great cultural influen became the official language. Many cou tries adopted everything British—good a bad. The British system of law, governme civil service and the class system were ported to widely differing cultures.

Britain was the first country to indust alize on a large scale. Most modern ind trial machinery owes some debt to Briti inventors.

Emigrants from Britain have spread ov the globe taking the British spirit with the North America, Australia and New Zeala have been built to some extent by har British pioneers.

Britain still ranks fourth in world trad London is a major financial centre. Brit maintains a naval and military presence many parts of the world and has a seat the security council of the United Natio Though Britain has a new role she is s making a positive contribution to wo culture, and to economic, military, a scientific affairs. The invisible forces British culture are most enduring of influences—for everyone who speaks En lish undergoes a British influence.

Where English is spoken

Canada

United Kingdom

U.S.A.

Jamaica
Barbados
Trinidad
Guyana

Australia

Tasmania

New Zealand

■ English spoken

□ English with other languages

Other language groups throughout the world (in millions)

Chinese 782m.	Spanish 195m.	Arabic 115m.
English 312m.	Indonesian 127m.	Japanese 108m.	Portuguese 75m.
Hindi 196m.	Russian 126m.	German 90m.	French 65m.

A French view of British influence over Egypt in 1893. During the 19th century Britain greatly enlarged her Empire and overseas interests. Egypt came under British protection in 1883, an event bitterly resented by the French as Egypt was the key to the Suez Canal. Britain did rather better than most powers in asserting her influence throughout the world.

Captain Cook discovers Australia in 1770. British explorers, from Drake to Scot, have been in the forefront of exploration.

Some British influences on the world

▲ The British have maintained a reputation for inventions from steam power to radar.

▲ English literature has a world-wide fame as the production of a Zulu version of Shakespeare's *Macbeth* shows.

▲ British products have a reputation for quality and sturdy construction.

▲ The British Parliamentary tradition has been established in many parts of the world.

▲ The London Stock Exchange has long had a powerful effect on financial dealings throughout the world.

▲ Organized trade unions began in Britain, then spread throughout the world.

▼ British people have carried their language and culture to every continent of the world.

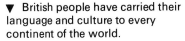

Home life

Pride in ownership

Home ownership is a British ideal, and the notion of "home" usually means a house with its own front door, a garden and a place to wash the car. Property prices are very high, so most people who do "own" their home have to repay heavy loans. Flats, seldom a feature of British home life in the past have become more common and local government housing has increased. Council estates, with flats and houses laid out among landscaped gardens, have provided lower rent housing for millions of people.

The typical style for older housing is the two-up-and-two-down terrace: a street of identical houses, each with two rooms on each of its two floors. Streets of terraced houses are found all over Britain. The building material varies according to the locality and the age of the street. These streets can look monotonous and poor, but behind the curtains the story can be different. Interiors are often bright and cheerful, decorated according to individual taste, though the age and social class of the inhabitants play a part.

Respect for privacy

British homes are informal, and hospitable. However, privacy is respected, especially in the south. Members of the family lead their own lives, sometimes only meeting for major meals and to watch television in the evening. This trend is increasing as more mothers go out to work. Children have the run of the house. Families where children are seen and not heard have become much less common.

Many households have a pet. The most popular are cats, dogs, budgerigars and tropical fish. In northern England pigeons are sometimes kept, usually in the back garden, for racing.

▲ Terraced houses of all periods are found everywhere. The style of building was adopted because the British always wanted their own front doors, and objected to flats.

▼ Afternoon tea with cakes and sandwiches used to be a family ritual among the leisured classes in Britain. Today teas like the one shown here are usually for occasions when visitors call.

▼ Not every family has a garden, but those people who do usually give much of their leisure time to its maintenance. Gardens in towns and cities are usually small. A few people grow fruit and vegetables, while the majority cultivate a patch of grass with a border of roses and other flowers.

A typical family timetable

7.30   8.00   8.30   9.00   9.15   12.30   1.00   2.00   4.30   6.00   8.00   11.00

An average family budget

25% Food

14% Vehicles and transport

13% Housing

10% Services, repairs etc.

9% Clothing, footwear

9% Alcohol, tobacco

7% Durable goods

7% Other goods

6% Fuel, light

◄ British families usually have enough for their needs, and for a few luxuries. The second-biggest item of expenditure is the family car (costing up to £14 a week), a luxury, since few people *must* have one.

▲ Many people find kitchen breakfasts convenient. This family is breakfasting on a working day, so the meal is a simple matter of cereal, crumpets and tea. At weekends, breakfasts are often more elaborate.

Leisure and pleasure

Something for everyone

The British are very fortunate in the wide choice of leisure pursuits available to them. The countryside is always within reach and most people have nearby clubs, "pubs" (public houses), cinemas, dance-halls and sports facilities. Cultural activities range from amateur choral and music groups to the grand scale of opera, theatre and art in the capital. At weekends many people devote their time to gardening or driving to the nearest country spot or beach. When the weather is unkind, home decorating and board or card games are popular.

Leisure at home

The average working week is 35-40 hours (plus 5-6 hours travelling to and from work), so people have sufficient time to make good use of their leisure. Much of this time is spent at home, watching television, reading, listening to the radio or record player, playing musical instruments or entertaining friends. The British are also very interested in hobbies, many of which have a cultural or educational value. Painting, pottery, model building, car maintenance, woodwork and again music are popular pursuits demanding a high level of skill. In 1972 over two million adults attended non-vocational courses.

▲ "Pubs", or Public Houses, have been places of entertainment and relaxation in Britain for hundreds of years. The attraction is good beer and lighthearted companionship. Opening hours are limited and only persons of 18 years and over may drink alcohol.

How leisure time is spent

Watching television 97%

Gardening 64%

Playing with children 62%

Driving 58%

Home decorating 53%

Pub visiting 52%

Source: Central Statistical Office 1970

▲ The table gives the percentage of the population engaging in selected activities at least once a month. Television is the most popular home-based pastime.

► British parks are landscaped and tended in the "natural" style, imitating the wilds. Parks are viewed as a national right and you may often walk on the grass.

A typical weekday television programme (evening programmes only)

B.B.C. 1

5.15	The Monkees: American series
5.40	Adventures of Parsley: cartoon
5.45	National News
6.00	Nationwide: current affairs
6.50	Star Trek: science fiction adventure
7.40	It Ain't Half Hot Mum: comedy series
8.10	The Dragon's Opponent: war drama serial
9.00	Nine O'Clock News, Weather
9.25	Happy Ever After: comedy series
9.55	Golden Horizons: documentary
10.50	Midweek: news and current affairs programme
11.35	Late Night News, Weather
11.42	The Sky at Night: astronomy
12.12	Weather, Closedown

B.B.C. 2

5.25 p.m.	Open University
7.30	News summary, Weather
7.35	European Heritage: art review
8.30	Man Alive: documentary
9.00	Midweek Cinema: The Women
11.00	News Extra
11.30	Closedown

ITV (Commercial Channel)

5.20	The Untamed World: documentary on the Rockies
5.50	News
6.00	Today: current affairs
6.30	Cartoon
6.45	Crossroads: serial
7.00	Macmillan and Wife: adventure series
7.30	Coronation Street: serial
8.00	Spring and Autumn: comedy series
8.30	The Brontës of Haworth: play
9.30	How's Your Father: comedy series
10.00	News at Ten
10.30	Late Night Drama: play
11.00	Football: highlights from evening matches
11.55	Night Gallery: horror series
12.20	Go Forth and Multiply: programme on problems of world population
12.30	Closedown

▲ Working men's clubs are popular in industrial towns. Drinking, talking, cabarets and gambling are the great attractions. "Bingo", a game of chance played for prizes is very popular.

▲ Newspapers and magazines flourish in all towns and cities of Britain. Many are sold from temporary stalls near stations and bus stops. Magazines offering advice on cooking, home management, beauty and fashion are especially popular.

▼ Village fairs usually have their own amusement parks. Here at Towersey Fair, merry-go-rounds and big-wheels have been set up for the public holiday. The operators often live in caravans, and pack their equipment on to trailers.

A sporting nation

The amateur basis of sport

Most British sports began as games of the leisured classes of society. Football, for example, was first played in its present form at Cambridge University in 1848. Increased leisure for all has now made sport part of British life — both for participators and spectators. Schools are required by law to provide for physical education, therefore all Britons have some contact with sport from an early age.

Though professionalism has transformed major events, the basic character of British sport has been formed by the enthusiastic amateur. Many thousands spend a great deal of their leisure time organizing, teaching, training and participating in sport.

Television along with professionalism, has aroused increasing interest in such varied sports as golf, tennis, athletics and show-jumping.

▲ Fans of Liverpool Football Club cheer their team. Football is Britain's most popular sport. There are 129 professional clubs in Great Britain. International matches arouse great interest.

▲ A rugby football match between Wales and Japan. Two versions of the game are played — Rugby Union, with 15 players, and Rugby League with 13 players. Rugby League is played mostly in the north of England. In both there is no substitution, no padding or forward passing.

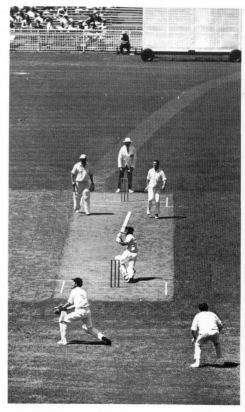

▶ Cricket, sometimes called the English national game, is known to have been played in some form from about 1550. Though games can take up to five days to complete, one-day matches have been recently introduced. The game is also played in Commonwealth countries.

THE BRITISH SPORTING YEAR

DEC. International Show Jumping, Wrestling, **Indoor Ice Figure Skating Championships**.

JAN. **English Table Tennis Championships**, Fencing, Skiing, Boxing.

FEB. Indoor athletics, **British Squash Championships**, Cyclo-Cross, **Indoor Tennis Championships**, ice skating.

MAR. **Grand National** steeplechase, "Flat" horse racing season starts, Cross Country Running Championships, Formula 1 auto racing starts, All England Badminton Championships, Oxford-Cambridge Boat Race.

APRIL Gymnastics Championships, Swimming trials, **Basketball Championships**, Judo Finals, Speedway starts, Cricket starts.

MAY **F.A. Cup Final** (soccer), **Rugby League Final**, **Cycle Tour of Britain**, **Amateur Boxing Finals**, **Home Internationals**

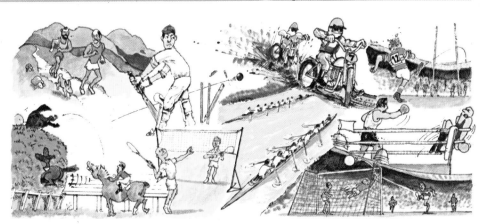

JUNE **The Derby** (Horse racing), **Wimbledon Fortnight Lawn Tennis Championships**, **Amateur Swimming Association Championships**, "Test" Cricket matches start, Isle of Man T.T. motor cycle races.

JULY **Henley Royal Regatta**, **British Open Golf Tournament**, **British Grand Prix** (Motor racing), **Amateur Athletics Championships**.

AUG. **Menai Straits Regatta, Cowes Week** (Yachting), **English Bowls Assoc. Championships**, Grouse and Snipe shooting begins, **International Power Boat Races**, Soccer resumes, Bisley Rifles.

SEPT. **Gillette Cup 1-day Cricket Finals**, Rugby resumes, Cricket ends..

OCT. **Horse-of-the-Year Show**, Pheasant season opens (hunting), Boxing, **Golf ends**.

NOV. Fox hunting season starts, RAC Motor Rally, End of "Flat" horse racing.

Holidays to suit everyone

▲ Holiday postcards range from views of scenery and architecture to the traditional seaside comic cards.

▼ Holiday "camps" at the seaside provide relatively cheap, organized holidays for millions. This Butlin's camp provides accommodation, meals and entertainment at pools, discos and shows of various kinds.

The seaside

British holidays have been revolutionized recent years by the "package deal" holida Cheap holidays in the sun lured many of t 8.5 million people who went abroad (main to Spain, France and Italy) in 1972. Hov ever the traditional British seaside holida begun 300 years ago, still retains its appea British resorts such as Blackpool a Brighton pride themselves on having a va variety of attractions from theatres on t pier to fun fairs. The beach itself is t greatest attraction in good weather. Boar ing houses, run by a "landlady" (who h become a figure of fun on comic postcard offer bed and breakfast at reasonable price

Competition with the seaside holiday h been provided since the 1930s by the holid camps. These aim to provide a comple holiday for up to 10,000 per camp, in an out of doors, by a vast range of entertai ments from organized sports to varie shows.

Taking the risk

Car ownership has made the British aware the variety of natural attractions through out their home country. Half of the 46 millio people who take a holiday every year, trave by car. Many go to the more remote parts Britain. Active holidays such as sailing canoeing, pony-trekking and camping ar increasing in popularity.

Holidays in Britain are, however, alway a gamble. It can rain in mid-summer or b scorching hot. Over 37 million peopl nevertheless, take the risk at least once year.

The main British holiday areas

Scottish Highlands
Orkney Is.
Lewis
Skye
Inverness
Grampian Mts.
Edinburgh
SCOTLAND
Welsh Mountains
Lake District
Yorkshire Dales
Isle of Man
Pennines
York
Lincoln
WALES
Cambrian Mts.
Norwich
Stratford on Avon
Ely
Cambridge
Cotswolds
Chiltern Hills
North Devon Coast
Bath
London
Margate
Ilfracombe
Brighton
Bude
Salisbury
Newquay
Dartmoor
Bognor Regis
St. Ives

Yorkshire Moors

Norfolk Broads

Houses of Parliament

Salisbury Cathederal

▲ Active holidays—camping, boating, walking and pony-trekking—are increasing in popularity. These campers have come by car to pitch their tents by the lake. Some walkers carry all their equipment on their backs in rucksacks, camping at different sites each night, others pack their gear onto bicycles, or into cars.

◀ Punch and Judy puppet shows were once a feature of beach entertainment. Punch is an irascible little man who swings his club at Judy (his wife), policemen and shopkeepers, but never quite masters the world.

▼ Boats in harbour at Ullapool, Scotland. Quiet fishing villages offer a different sort of holiday from the noisy, bustling seaside camps. Many people visit the same village each year; some permanently moor their boats in the harbour.

The changing face of education

Universal education

British parents are required by law to see that their children receive efficient full-time education, between the ages of 5 and 16. This principle of compulsory education was established in 1870 for England and Wales. Scotland has had a separate educational history and system but has followed the same lines. It was however some time before all children were being educated at least to primary level.

By 1972 there were 10.5 million school children at 37,490 schools. The vast majority were at state schools, but there are also thousands of independent schools outside the state system including the fee-paying "Public Schools" such as Eton and Harrow.

In Britain boys and girls are usually taught together in primary schools. In state secondary schools two-thirds of pupils in England and Wales are in mixed schools. In Scotland nearly all secondary schools are mixed.

A great debate

Secondary education is in a state of transition. The majority of pupils in England and Wales in 1972 were in schools to which they were allocated after taking an examination at 11 (the "11-Plus"). Those who passed it went to academic schools (called Grammar Schools) which were intended to prepare them for higher education. Those who failed went to "Secondary Modern Schools" giving a general education with a practical bias. Because of the many criticisms of this system by educationalists and politicians "Comprehensive" schools were introduced which take all pupils regardless of ability. A third of state pupils attended such schools in 1972. The issue is being hotly debated. The Labour Party is determined that all schools should go "comprehensive". Scottish schools are largely organized on comprehensive lines.

Britain has an extensive system of education beyond the secondary school from technical colleges to polytechnics and universities for the highest level of studies. The numbers in higher education have increased from 198,200 in 1961 to 472,000 in 1971. The majority of full-time students are entitled to maintenance grants.

▲ A modern secondary school in London. The newer school buildings are usually more spacious, better heated, and have better equipped classrooms and laboratories. In 1972-3 the State spent over £3,000 million on education.

◄ Girls in the classroom. Large classes and a shortage of teachers are a constant problem.

▼ A school chemistry laboratory. In this laboratory, each pupil has a bunsen burner, test tubes and chemicals to conduct experiments.

The educational system

Nursery (under 5 years)

Infant (5-7 years)

Junior (8-11 years)

Comprehensive (11-16 plus)

Grammar (11-16 plus)

Secondary Modern (11–16 plus)

Further education (16 plus)

Art, Drama and Music schools

University (18 plus)

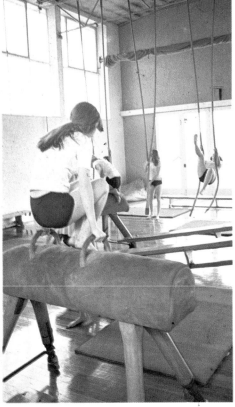

▲ A school gymnasium. Physical education, which includes games, is part of every school's curriculum.

► Kings College, Cambridge, one of the well-known colleges in the complex of Cambridge University. Oxford and Cambridge are the oldest British universities.

Shops and shopping

A nation of shopkeepers

Napoleon's gibe that the British were a race of shopkeepers was not kindly meant, but it contains a measure of truth. British power derived from buying and selling, often buying raw materials and selling finished goods. The British, with this experience behind them, are shrewd shoppers. They expect quality, and they have a good eye for bargains. Food is the biggest item in the family budget, and British shoppers resent having to pay high prices for it.

Distribution

Supermarkets (self service shops with a minimum selling area of 2,000 square feet) have spread rapidly and now handle a third of all retail food sales. They have taken trade from the independent grocers who are trying to fight back by joining groups. Groups buy in large quantities, and can thus keep prices as low as the supermarkets.

The development of supermarkets has encouraged lavish packaging. The shopper faced, for instance, with five brands of washing powder, will often chose the best packed, believing that the smartest box must contain the best detergent. Recently shoppers have begun to protest about the high price of excessive packaging.

▲ Giant retail houses owning many shops are found in every high street. Woolworth sell a wide range of cheap goods.

▼ The milkman's "float", an electric van. Britain is one of the few places where milk is delivered to your door.

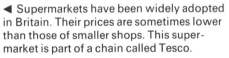

▲ A display of fruit on a street market stall. Stallkeepers (known as "barrow boys") have to rise very early to buy their supplies from the wholesale market.

◀ Supermarkets have been widely adopted in Britain. Their prices are sometimes lower than those of smaller shops. This supermarket is part of a chain called Tesco.

▲ Antiques and period silverware are popular in Britain, and many people enjoy browsing through markets or junkshops in the hope of finding bargains.

▼ Carnaby Street, on the edge of Soho, London, rose to fame in the 1960s as a centre for casual fashionable clothes. Now the Carnaby styles are universal.

Eating the British way

Typical meals for a day

The workday breakfast usually consists of cornflakes, toast and tea.

Lunch is often a quick meal of sausages and beans, with tea or coffee.

Evening dinner is the main meal of the day. Steak and kidney pudding with potatoes and green vegetables is a favourite main course.

Changing habits

British food had, until recently, an undeserved reputation for dullness. During and shortly after the war many foods were in short supply, and plain meals became the norm. Elizabethan cookery was celebrated, and Edwardians were famous for their enormous meals. According to legend people ate breakfast till 10.30 a.m., followed by a solid lunch, a big tea, dinner with twelve or more courses and a late night supper. After Edwardian times meals became smaller, fewer and simpler.

Today the elaborate ritual of high tea is disappearing, and a main evening meal is replacing the noontime dinner. Home cooking in Britain has always been wholesome. By tradition, northerners eat better than southerners and the Scots eat least well, though recently standards have risen everywhere with increased interest in food and wine.

Sunday dinner

One tradition which has remained unshakeable is the Sunday roast, eaten in the middle of the day. Occasionally cheaper meat like roast lamb or chicken is the main course, but roast beef is considered the proper Sunday dinner. Special features are the roasted potatoes and Yorkshire pudding. Yorkshire pudding needs flair; in the wrong hands it can turn out doughy. At its best, it is light and fluffy, completing a dish you can even offer to a Frenchman.

▲ The cheeses of Britain are mostly on the solid side. Cheddar and Stilton are the best known. Cheese with onions and bread makes a Ploughman's lunch which may be modest, but is tasty and nourishing.

Some regional dishes

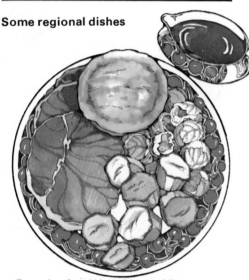

▲ Roast beef and Yorkshire pudding, or "Pud", is a traditional main course. Popular taste is for the meat to be well done when eaten hot, less so when cold. The accompanying vegetables are likely to be potatoes, carrots, peas or sprouts.

▲ Haggis is the Scottish speciality which is either venerated or loathed. It is solemnly served on Burns' Night. Haggis consists of sheep's liver, suet, onions, oatmeal and seasoning. It is stuffed into a sheep's stomach, and steamed for a couple of hours.

▲ Leeks and cheese with ham is a simple enough Welsh dish. The leek is the national badge of the Welsh and is worn in their hats on St. David's Day. Another Welsh speciality is the Welsh Rarebit or Rabbit, with eggs and cheese on toast.

Make yourself a meal

MIXED VEGETABLE SOUP
1 lb. mixed vegetables
1 oz. fat
2 pints stock
Bouquet garni and seasoning
1 oz. oatmeal or oats
¼ pint milk
Parsley

Mince the vegetables. Melt the fat and
sauté them briefly. Add the stock,
seasoning and bouquet garni. Simmer
over a low heat until the vegetables are
tender. Then stir in the oatmeal or rolled
oats with milk and cook for 10 minutes
more. Add chopped parsley when
serving.

SHEPHERD'S PIE
1 lb. potatoes
2 teaspoons of milk
½ oz. butter or margarine
An onion, chopped
Dripping or lard
½ lb. minced meat (cooked)
Stock, herbs and seasoning

Boil the potatoes, strain, then mash,
adding milk, butter, salt and pepper. Fry
the onion in dripping or lard, mix with
the minced meat, stock, seasoning and
herbs. Put the mashed potatoes in a pie
dish and fill the middle with the meat
mixture. Cover the top with mashed
potato and heat in a medium oven for
half an hour.

BAKED APPLES AND CUSTARD
4 medium-sized cooking apples
1 tablespoon golden syrup
1 oz. brown sugar 2 oz. dried fruit
Wash apples and cut out cores, using an
apple corer or small knife. Fill hole in
each apple with syrup, sugar and dried
fruit. Place in greased dish with a little
water and bake in medium oven till tender.
Custard
2 tablespoons custard powder
1 oz. sugar, 1 pint cold milk
Few drops of vanilla essence
Blend custard powder with a little milk
until smooth. Heat rest of milk and when
hot but not boiling pour onto powder mix.
Return mixture to pan and bring to boil,
stirring all the time. Add sugar and
vanilla essence. Serve.

▲ Whelks, cockles, mussels and eels are
traditional Cockney seafoods. Seafood
stalls offer a cheap snack on the street.

◀ Fish and chip shops provide another
traditional food. They offer quick service
and a solid meal at a cheap price.

A genius for drama

▲ William Shakespeare (1564-1616). This is the nearest we have to an authentic portrait. Little is known about his life.

▶ The Globe Theatre as it might have looked on London's south bank at Southwark. It was almost a theatre-in-the-round, with little scenery, no footlights, no lighting, and no roof.

Shakespeare's best-known plays

Shakespeare's plays are often grouped into tragedies, comedies and histories (historical plays). Most British people have seen or read half a dozen or so of the plays; a Shakespeare fan will at least know the most popular plays listed below:

Tragedies
Romeo and Juliet
Julius Caesar
Hamlet
Othello
King Lear
Macbeth
Anthony and Cleopatra

Comedies
A Midsummer Night's Dream
Much Ado About Nothing
As You Like It
Twelfth Night
The Tempest

Histories
Richard III
Henry IV (Parts 1 and 2)
Henry V

Shakespeare—Bard of Avon

Britain is a literary nation. There have been important British musical composers, painters and architects, but it is in literature that British arts have reached their highest point. Within literature, drama claims the first attention, because one sublime playwright and poet raised the drama to unprecedented heights. Shakespeare's plays combine action and excitement of plot with magnificent language and a deep knowledge of the human heart.

In Shakespeare's time the drama was already flourishing. The Elizabethan and Jacobean ages were self-confident and swaggering; blood-and-thunder playwrights like Kidd and Marlowe were creating a tradition which Shakespeare adapted to his own passionate and melancholy genius. During the Protectorate drama was banned. After the Restoration of the Monarchy, which followed in 1660, dramatists revealed another of the masks of drama: Congreve and Farquhar wrote plays and elegant satire suited to the more urbane culture of their day.

The tradition of English drama

Today the tradition continues. More plays are written than even the most dedicated of theatres could produce. Modern playwrights still deal with the preoccupations of Shakespeare, portraying the inadequacies, absurdities and suffering that rise from our human condition and life in society. Films, a related art form, are facing serious economic problems. British television shows many British plays and films. Of all artforms in Britain today, drama is probably the most widely appreciated.

▲ Scene from an early production of *Wife for a Month* a tragi-comedy by the Jacobean dramatists Beaumont and Fletcher.

◄ Sir Laurence Olivier is one of Britain's most famous actor-managers. Here he plays the part of Shylock, the Jewish moneylender, in a production of *The Merchant of Venice* staged in Victorian costume.

▼ The New National Theatre under construction on London's south bank of the River Thames. There are over 270 professional theatres in Britain, including nearly 60 companies providing programmes for children and young people.

▲ William Congreve (1670-1729), poet and playwright, was a leading figure in post-Restoration drama. His wit exposed the affectations of people attempting to shine in society.

▲ John Osborne, author of *Look Back in Anger*, first produced in 1956. Osborne became the leader of a group of playwrights called "The Angry Young Men". Their plays of social realism depicted the struggles of poor and inarticulate urban people.

A passion for expression

The Renaissance and after

Britain has a great artistic tradition descending from the culture of classical Greece and Rome. The English Renaissance of the fifteenth and sixteenth centuries put Britain among the leading artistic nations. Allowing for a few lapses, it has remained there ever since.

Literature is the most famous area. Here writers have made full use of a great national advantage: a musical, heavily accented, flexible language, superbly exploited by Chaucer, Donne, Milton, Pope, Keats, and many other poets. The novel is the second area of literary fame. Dostoevsky, the great Russian novelist, for instance, frankly acknowledged his debt to London's Charles Dickens, referring to Dickens as the "master". The books of writers like Dickens, Jane Austen, George Eliot (Mary Ann Evans), Thomas Hardy, can be read again and again without losing their interest.

Painting and Music

Painting is an old art in Britain, though famous artists date only from Tudor times and it was only after the eighteenth century that British painting achieved international recognition. Hogarth, Reynolds, Constable, Gainsborough and Turner are best known, though not by any means the only important British painters.

British musicians and painters have learnt much from continental Europe. One of Britain's major composers, George Frederick Handel, came from Bavaria. Purcell, Holst, and Vaughan Williams are important British composers, creators of a tradition further developed today by Benjamin Britten, and Michael Tippett.

Today British arts are in a state of ferment, partly caused by rapid change in technology and upheaval and bewilderment in society. Since the First World War many established values have been questioned and artists have been foremost among the critics. Experiment in new forms of expression has preoccupied many artists, while others attempt to remake links with the past, adapting it to an uncertain but exciting present.

▲ Lincoln Cathedral begun in 1192 is considered by many to be the finest English Cathedral.

▼ A detail from Peace, a modern stained glass window in Canterbury Cathedral, made in an English tradition 700 years old.

▲ The Angel of Destruction, painted by William Blake (1757-1827), poet, painter and visionary. Blake ignored the polished conventions of the eighteenth century; his poems and paintings have a forcefulness unique in British art.

► Charles Dickens (1812-70), the prolific Victorian novelist whose characters are among the best-loved of English fiction.

▼ Joseph Mallord William Turner (1775-1851) used semi-abstract techniques to express the forces of nature. He was fascinated by the power of light as this picture of the Fighting Téméraire being towed to her last berth (1839) shows.

▲ Robert Burns (1759-96), the national poet of Scotland. This statue appropriately shows Burns as a young man, for his Scottish humour has a youthful quality.

▼ Benjamin Britten (born 1913) is one of the world's leading modern composers. The picture shows a scene from his opera Gloriana about Queen Elizabeth I.

The inventive British

"If at first you don't succeed..."

The British love invention—from messing about in boats to the advanced developments of wireless and telescopes. When this was turned to industrial use as early as 1712 with Newcomen's steam engine to pump water from mines, a new era began. From 1761, canals developed industrial communications, which were carried forward by Stephenson's railroads and bridges. Much of this was made possible by the development of the steam engine.

New roads by Telford and McAdam "speeded" a process which has been going on since Tudor times—private enterprise developed, and huge factories were able to produce goods in large quantities.

The English "invented" industry, and the industrial town. It was in England, too, that the first trade unions were established.

British ingenuity

British ingenuity is found in a wide variety of fields. London was the world's first giant metropolis through early developments in omnibuses, trams, and the underground railway or tube.

Steamships were another British innovation; the first to cross the Atlantic was the "Savannah"; it crossed in 1818. The next year saw the first airship that really worked (top speed 9 km., $5\frac{1}{2}$ miles per hour). Agriculture also soon went over to steam, and mechanized many farming processes. Britain was the first country to turn its peasants into "farmworkers".

Medical progress owes much to Britain, as do physics, electronics, aeronautics and engineering which have led to innovations such as the hovercraft and the first supersonic airliners.

The Rocket—a 29 m.p.h. miracle

▲ Isaac Newton (1642-1727) splitting light with a prism. Newton made many contributions to scientific knowledge, among them the law of gravity and the Newton telescope. In life this great mathematician was gentle and unassuming. When his dog knocked over a lamp, causing a fire which destroyed years of work, Newton merely told his dog sadly that it would never know what it had done to its master

▶ George Stephenson (1781-1848), a miner's son, pioneered the first steam locomotive railway between Stockton and Darlington in 1825. Previously animals had been used on railways for hauling coal between the pithead and ports. His locomotive, called *Locomotion*, was to draw the first public passenger train in the world. Stephenson went on to design and build the *Rocket* (right) which was used on the new Liverpool and Manchester railway.

▲ Michael Faraday (1791-1867) made advances in chemistry, physics and electricity. The development of electrical engineering can be traced back to his discovery of electro-magnetic induction in 1831. The principle of the electric motor, the dynamo, the transformer and the telephone were first demonstrated by his experiments. Faraday is considered by many to have been the world's greatest experimental genius.

▶ Charles Darwin (1809-82) never said that humans descended from monkeys, yet many people thought he had. His *Origin of Species* published in 1859 was thought atheistic and was vigorously attacked. Now Darwin's theory of evolution is widely accepted.

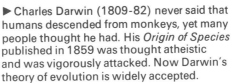

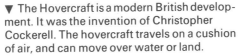

▼ The Hovercraft is a modern British development. It was the invention of Christopher Cockerell. The hovercraft travels on a cushion of air, and can move over water or land.

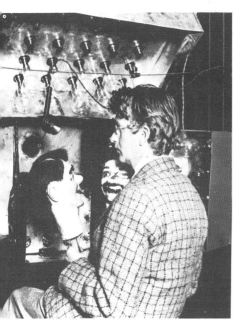

▲ John Logie Baird, the Scottish engineer, was responsible for the first public T.V. picture of September 30, 1929. He was the unpaid hero of the dawn of T.V., for seven years later when regular public service was started by the British Broadcasting Corporation, his process was soon abandoned. In 1939 Baird gave a demonstration of television in natural colours.

Products for the world

Export or die

Britain is a small island with a large urban population. It does not produce enough food to feed everybody, and has to supply its 54 million people with a wide range of consumer goods. So Britain must import much of the food and raw materials that it lacks. Britain has to sell its own products abroad to pay for these imports. To survive, Britain really must "export or die".

Manufactured goods head the list. Britain is a major producer of machinery, aircraft, cars, ships and steel. Chemicals and textiles are also very important among export products.

The wool industry has been centred in Yorkshire, in the north-east of England, since the early days of mechanical wool weaving. Yorkshire's grassy hills are suitable for sheep raising, and there is an abundant supply of soft water for processing. Cotton cloth, made from fibres imported through Liverpool, and synthetic fabric, are made in Lancashire, Yorkshire's rival county in the west. Scotland produces tweeds woven by hand in traditional styles. London is another centre, in this case of the "rag trade", for London design and fashion have a reputation for fun and flair.

Cars, aircraft and ships

British transport manufacturers—of cars, aircraft and ships—now operate in a highly competitive sphere. Design has to be changed frequently to keep pace with mechanical improvements and changes in taste. Every change means new machinery, a very expensive item for hard-pressed manufacturers. None the less, British goods have kept their reputation for craftsmanship. Hardy lightweights like the "Mini", as much as powerful locomotive engines maintain this reputation.

▲ A steel furnace in Wales. Steel is the basis of many British industries, so its production is of national importance.

▼ Coal was the major fuel used in British industry, and still provides electricity, manufactured gas, coke, and many by-products. These miners are drilling holes for explosives in the rock face.

Some major British industrial products

▲ British cars are a major export product, and much in demand at home.

▲ Chemical products are another giant pillar of the British economy. In 1973 10% of British exports were chemicals.

How whisky is made

Highland burn

Wet barley being turned on the malting floor

The grist being mixed in the mash tun

Pot stills

Distillation being controlled from the spirit safe

The new whisky is pumped into a spirit vat then into oak casks

Malt and grain whiskies are left to mature in oak casks

▲ Scottish whisky ("Scotch" for short) is made in vast quantities, but by methods used for centuries. The basic ingredient is barley. This is cleaned, then soaked in the Highland's famous water till it softens. Later it is dried in the malt kiln and crushed into "grist". The grist is mixed with hot water, and the sweet liquid (called "wort") drained off. This wort is fermented, then distilled in copper pot stills. The new whisky from the still is left to mature in oak casks for several years. It is usually blended and then bottled.

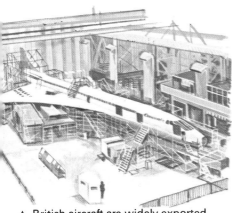

▲ British aircraft are widely exported. "Concorde" (shown here) is a pioneering venture sponsored by Britain and France.

▲ Textiles (natural and synthetic) are a traditional product, high among Britain's exports.

▲ Pottery is an ancient craft, as old as civilization. British pottery is still made in many traditional styles. Crockery is mass-produced in factories, and also made by small cottage potters who turn the clay on a pedal-wheel and fire it in their home kilns. Here skilled craftspeople are painting in a design.

London the complete city

The founding of London

The Romans established London (Londinium) at the beginning of the Christian era. It has been Britain's main city ever since. Its location on the river Thames secured its importance first as a port, later as a commercial centre. London has had a violent history. It has been burned or sacked at least five times; it has provided good pickings for criminals and has always had a strong attraction for ambitious, dissatisfied young Britons from the country.

There were farms near the centre until quite recent years. Some areas still retain a village-like atmosphere. However, traffic congestion is now a menace and rents are high. London, big as it is, bustles with its nine million people who all seem to be out in the streets at the same time.

The Londoners

During its long history, London has absorbed many outlying villages. Hampstead, for instance, was a village in the eighteenth century. Cockneys are still considered to be the "real" Londoners. Anyone born within the sound of the bells of Bow Church, near Fleet Street, the newspaper headquarters, is a Cockney.

There are many other London types, London ways and London accents, just as there are many Londons. The City, the oldest part, is still the nation's financial centre. Most theatres are concentrated in the West End, the nightlife capital, abutting on Soho, famous for its restaurants. Chelsea, once a poor area, has a "swinging" reputation, but living there is almost as expensive as in elegant Kensington and Belgravia. Other areas, like Notting Hill and the inner East End, offer a refuge for young, single workers, students and immigrants from Commonwealth countries.

London with its many museums, traditional buildings, and numerous parks, requires a lifetime to explore.

▼ London became the largest city in the world 50 years after the Great Fire of 1666 and Dr. Samuel Johnson's words still apply "When a man is tired of London, he is tired of life".

Things to see in London

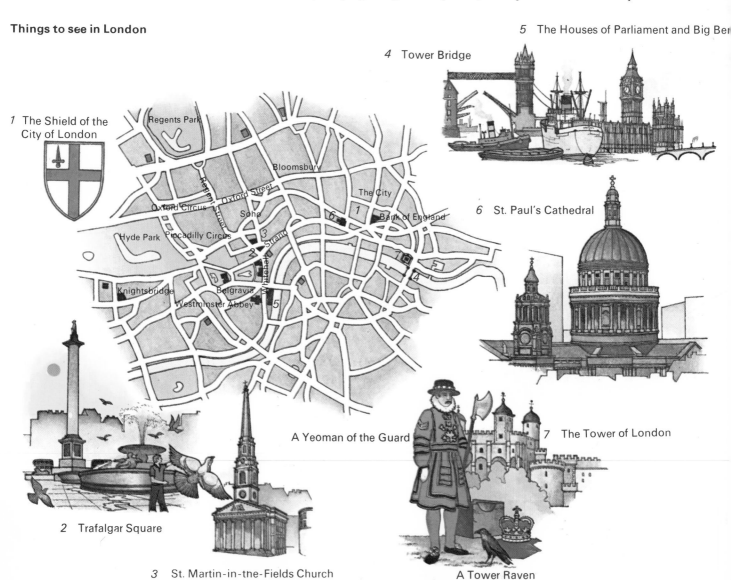

1 The Shield of the City of London

2 Trafalgar Square

3 St. Martin-in-the-Fields Church

4 Tower Bridge

5 The Houses of Parliament and Big Ben

6 St. Paul's Cathedral

7 The Tower of London

A Yeoman of the Guard

A Tower Raven

▲ The Serpentine lake in Hyde Park is only a mile from the very centre, but it can feel like the country.

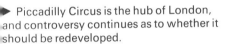

► Piccadilly Circus is the hub of London, and controversy continues as to whether it should be redeveloped.

▲ The City, seen from Waterloo Bridge, which spans the River Thames. St. Paul's Cathedral, masterpiece of the architect Christopher Wren, still dominates the skyline of this oldest and most intensively developed part of London. The Thames is navigable by smaller ocean-going vessels though today many of the craft are pleasure-boats.

▲ Buskers, or street singers, are a London speciality. Buskers sing to cinema queues and in public subways. They make a modest living from the passing crowds.

The monarchy today

Beginnings of the monarchy

The monarchy arose in Britain during the Dark Ages. By the time of Alfred the Great (902), the kingdom had grown to include most of England. Wales was annexed in 1282. Scotland became part of Britain much later, in 1603. The wily Queen Elizabeth I solved the ancient feud between the kingdoms of England and Scotland by leaving her crown to "our cousin of Scotland". He became King James I (of England) and VI (of Scotland).

For centuries the monarchs were engaged in a contest for power with the barons (the powerful landlords) and the church. The kings and barons reached a settlement in 1215. King John, who was temporarily at the mercy of his barons, was forced to sign a document, the Magna Carta ("Great Charter"). This charter limited the power of the king.

This sharing of power took a different form in later years. Rich merchants gradu-ally became more influential than the aristocracy. Parliament, which voiced t merchants' needs, whittled away the roy power. At one period, the struggle erup into civil war. King Charles I was execut and the monarchy abolished between 16 and 1660. Then the dead king's son w invited to fill the vacant throne as Char II. The last monarch to make a serio attempt to control Parliament was Geor III. Since his death in 1820, monarchs ha "reigned, but not ruled"

Queen Elizabeth II

Elizabeth II has reigned since 1953. She Head of State, and no Act of Parliame can become law without her consent. She also head of the English Church. She h many ceremonial duties. Major state of casions are given character and dignity I traditional pageantry The Queen is t main actor in many of these sometimes ve exhausting ceremonies.

◀ Horseguards outside Buckingham Palace, the London home of Her Majesty the Queen. When the Queen is in residence a flag is flown above the palace.

▼ The Coronation in 1953 of Her Majesty Queen Elizabeth II was heralded as the beginning of another Elizabethan age. The The Coronation ceremony, at Westminster Abbey, followed the tradition laid down by generations of crownings. Britain, colonies and countries of the commonwealth portrayed the new Queen on postage stamps.

▲ Trooping the Colour, the attractive public ceremony at the Horseguards' Parade off Pall Mall near Buckingham Palace in Londor Guardsmen sometimes faint in the heat, and the Queen has to display her best horseman-

The Royal Standard (the lions of England, the Welsh harp and the lion of Scotland)

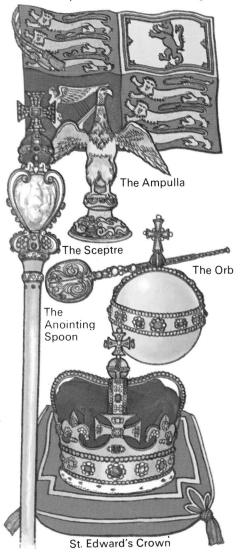

The Ampulla

The Sceptre

The Orb

The Anointing Spoon

St. Edward's Crown

▲ The Investiture of Prince Charles as Prince of Wales took place at Caernarvon Castle, Wales, in 1969. Prince Charles, heir to the British throne, has learnt to speak the Welsh language.

▶ The regalia of the British monarchy on display at the Tower of London. The ensign and these emblems of royalty represent the rights and privileges of royalty.

▼ The Queen on tour, in the West Indies, 1966. She is head of the Commonwealth. Britain has many historic, cultural and economic links with her former colonies.

hip. It is one of the most popular events in he tourist season and is held annually on the Queen's Official Birthday in June. Here the Queen (left foreground) rides side-saddle, while inspecting the troops.

The Elizabethan splendour

Good Queen Bess

Elizabeth I, queen of England and Wales from 1558-1603, was a remarkable ruler. She was the first British monarch to give her name to an age. Hers was a glittering and vital age at that. Elizabeth, the younger daughter of Henry VIII, had genius, courage, scholarship, learning and the foresight to set England on its course towards greatness. She was revered even by those who suffered under her, like the man whose arm was taken off and is said to have waved the stump, crying "God bless the Queen". Elizabeth was a ruthless politician. She executed her cousin, Mary the deposed Queen of Scots, who was a Catholic and a focus of Catholic disaffection with her Protestant policy. She faced a divided country, bitterly racked with religious strife, and a depleted treasury. She triumphed over both, as well as many attempted rebellions.

Troubles at home

While the sea dogs Drake, Grenville, Raleigh and Hawkins were opening the world to English trade and conquest, at home there were wars in Scotland and Ireland, and serious troubles over religion. Elizabeth's father, Henry VIII, had declared the independence of the English Church from Rome, and Elizabeth inherited the conflict. The Pope excommunicated the British Protestant monarchs, and told British Catholics that they were under no obligation to obey a ruler expelled from the church. Elizabeth was in serious danger of a Catholic rebellion.

Nonetheless, her court was merry with "pastimes", and there was a great outburst of artistic activity—writers like Shakespeare, Bacon, Spenser, Marlowe and Ben Jonson, architects like Inigo Jones, and a host of musicians including Campion and Morley. Work and play was hard. Elizabeth was the last of the great Tudor monarchs. When she died in 1603 the world looked both more peaceful and smaller. Sir Francis Drake had sailed round it, 25 years earlier, under Elizabeth's patronage. Elizabeth, unlike her great captains and explorers, never set foot outside Britain; and she never married.

▲ Sir Walter Raleigh (c. 1552-1618) rose to high favour through his daring naval leadership, exploration in America and flashy gallantry.

The great voyages of discovery

Willoughby & Chancellor 1553
Willoughby 1553
Varzino
Chancellor 1553
1555
Moscow
Davis 1587
Frobisher 1576-77
Newfoundland
Gilbert 1583
Raleigh's Virginia Colony 1585
St. Augustine
Drake 1572-73
Madeira
Canary Is.
Cuba
San Juan de Ulua
Hispaniola
Trinidad
Hawkins 1566
Margarita
Borburata
Rio de la Hacha
Santa Marta
Cartagena
Hawkins 1567-69
Sierra Leone (Slave Coast)
Drake 1579
ATLANTIC OCEAN

◄ The Warwick portrait of the Virgin Queen. Elizabeth was tall, red-haired, impressive, and a very firm ruler.

▼ Philip II of Spain sent the Armada to invade England in 1588. The English navy was better led and its small ships were more agile. The Spaniards were put to flight.

▲ Mary Stuart, Queen of Scots, Elizabeth's cousin, was executed in 1587. Elizabeth ordered her death with reluctance, for her cousin was an anointed queen—but Mary was a Catholic and a focus of discontent with Elizabeth's Protestant government.

▲ The Tower of London, much used as a political prison in Elizabeth's time. Elizabeth herself was briefly held there during her half-sister Mary Tudor's reign. "Beefeaters", guardians of the Tower and its treasures, once inspired fear.

The great age of Victoria

Wealth and power

Victoria acted like a great monarch, even though her powers were limited. Her husband, Prince Albert, tried to do the same, but was constantly rebuffed. Albert was a German, and the British never quite accepted him.

Britain's Victorian age was remarkable for the expansion in wealth and power. Paradoxically, it was also the first age of the common man. Victorian England is remembered for its appalling slums—not because they were new to the great cities, but because the press and public leaders began to notice them, and because the poor themselves began to work for change. Education was seen as the great instrument of social reform; many schools were built. Some Victorian morality does now seem hypocritical, but huge changes were taking place behind this sober facade. Industry was replacing agriculture as the basis of the economy; the British were becoming an urban people. Engineering innovations followed one another with bewildering speed, and the old aristocracy and gentry lost their power to the new middle class.

Victoria's role

The Queen understood the arts of government. So although her Prime Ministers, Palmerston, Disraeli and Gladstone wielded the real power, she remained in close touch with political developments. She and Prince Albert patronized artists, encouraged the spread of education and the building of museums so that people who could not own national treasures individually could at least share them, as citizens.

Victoria's popularity was high throughout her reign of 63 years. When she died in 1901 the whole nation went into mourning. Perhaps people sensed that, after Victoria, the ferment in society and among nations would break through the surface. The post-Victorian world experienced war and destruction, as well as an era of prosperity for richer nations on a scale unknown before.

▼ In the early hours of the morning, on June 20, 1837, Victoria was woken to be told that William IV had died, and she was queen. Victoria, then 17 years old, heard the news with dignity, as this romantic portrait shows. She is said to have been unaware, until aged twelve, that she would succeed to the throne. On hearing the news she is reported to have said, "I will be good."

▲ The Charge of the Light Brigade in the Crimean War against Russia (1854-6) was a military blunder. The troops knew the charge would be suicide, but were ordered to advance regardless. Out of 673, 113 were killed and 134 wounded.

▲ The Albert Memorial still stands as a testimony to Victoria's grief for her husband, Prince Albert, who died in December 1861.

▶ A historic photograph of the Royal Family showing Victoria with the later Edward VII, George V and Edward VIII.

▼ The darker side of Victorian life in slums of 1860s. There was a vast gulf between rich and poor.

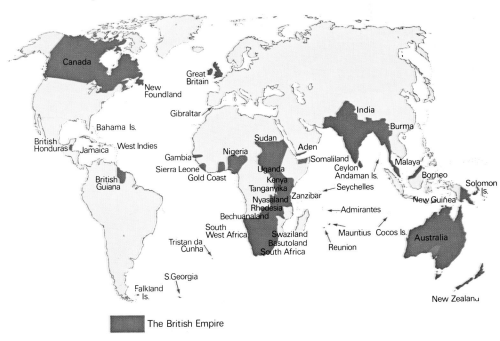

The British Empire 1919

The British Empire

▲ The British Empire reached its greatest extent shortly after Victorias reign. However, even during the Queen's lifetime it received one serious shock. The Boers rebelled twice and challenged the Empire for two years. They were finally quelled in 1901

Winston Churchill man of the century

The soldier-politician

Churchill always had a fighting spirit; even as a boy he had a passion for war games and tin soldiers. By the time he was 26, he had seen three minor wars, been a war correspondent, authored two large volumes and lost his first election. Not much later he was a Member of Parliament who had switched parties (from Conservative to Liberal), been a hero of the Boer War and become a national figure. By the time he was 40, he was First Lord of the Admiralty. He then built up the fleet to be ready for the war which he believed to be inevitable.

The fleet was ready in 1914 but a defeat over the Gallipoli campaign in 1915 forced him to resign.

During the peace that followed, he held some state positions, but his aggressive temperament made him ill-suited to the problems of peace. Serious blunders in his dealings with the trade unions, especially during the General Strike in 1926, revealed his lack of sympathy with the aims of the poorer working people.

Churchill's brand of politics had little appeal during the 1930s and he held no government post. He was, however, watching the growing menace of Germany and preparing for his greatest challenge.

In 1940 he finally achieved his ambition of becoming Prime Minister. The Second World War had already begun, and Churchill's positive, bulldog-like leadership was just what the nation needed.

"We shall never surrender"

Churchill's wartime speeches and energy were legendary. Britain, he declared, would never surrender. His cigar and V-for-victory sign caught the imagination of millions. Yet at the first election after victory, Churchill was badly defeated and a Labour government came to power. The welfare state was created without him.

In 1951 he again became Prime Minister, till he resigned in 1955, aged 81. He died ten years later, and was honoured with a state funeral. Characteristically, he had planned all its details.

▲ Winston Churchill in 1895, a subaltern in the 4th Hussars. Lord Randolph Churchill hoped that his son would become a barrister but young Winston wanted an active life and chose an army career.

◄ Churchill with Lloyd George in 1915, during World War One. Churchill was then First Lord of the Admiralty. In that year Churchill backed the Gallipoli campaign— an attempt to attack Germany from behind. The campaign was a failure. Churchill, as a result, returned to soldiering for a while.

▲ Armoured cars escorting a food convoy during the general strike, 1926. Churchill opposed any compromise with the strikers. Churchill was never forgiven for his hostility to the strikers. He edited a government-sponsored newspaper, The British Gazette, which was a focus for anti-strike agitation.

▲ The evacuation of British forces from Dunkirk, 1940. France fell to the German advance, and the British forces had to retreat very quickly. Little ships of all kinds rushed across the Channel where they picked up the soldiers under heavy German fire.

▼ St. Paul's Cathedral was ringed by fire during bombing raids on London in the last war. It survived, and so did Britain, with a fighting spirit that Churchill embodied so strongly. Many people lost their homes during the air raids.

▲ Churchill was in and out of public life throughout his career. His statue in Parliament Square, Westminster, shows him as an old statesman. When he died, it did seem truly to be the end of an era.

Heroes of fact and fiction

The great tradition

The British have a rich tradition of heroes, both real and fictional. Bravery, determination, wit and chivalry are much admired qualities. A long line of heroes can be traced back from King Arthur and his Knights of the Round Table through to James Bond. All are struggling against evil forces to defend a personal code of honour. Alfred the Great and Robert the Bruce fought to expel invaders. Robin Hood was against the unscrupulous King John. Sir Francis Drake defeated the Armada for Queen and Country. Sherlock Holmes and the numerous other fictional detectives sought to bring justice. The British prefer their heroes to succeed but forgive them if they have done their best. Military heroes such as Wolfe, Wellington and Nelson would probably have been forgotten if they had failed.

Also admired is the inventive and dashing criminal. Dick Turpin, a highwayman, captured the imagination by his string of daring robberies and desperate attempts to escape. The 1963 "Great Train Robbery", in which £2,595,998 was stolen, is admired by people who wouldn't like to be robbed themselves. The British have always had an affection for the underdog but he must have the ability to win in the end.

▲ King Arthur battles with his supporter Sir Accolon, due to a deception of Queen Morgana le Fay. Sir Accolon, given Arthur's magic sword Excalibur, believed himself to be fighting an enemy. Excalibur, the great sword, would have been the death of Arthur, but another magician, Lady Nimue, enchanted the sword out of Accolon's hand. King Arthur and his knights, dedicated to the ideals of chivalry and honour, are among the most important British heroes.

▶ Friar Tuck became "Chaplain" to the outlaw of Sherwood Forest, Robin Hood, and his Merrie Men, after a contest of strength and wits. Robin and the hermit Friar took turns in carrying each other across a stream, for neither would be the last to get his feet wet. The Friar ended the contest by tipping Robin into the water. Friar Tuck joined the Merrie Men, for he was as fond of poaching game and of robbing the rich to feed the poor, as any of the band.

◄ Sherlock Holmes was the creation of Sir Arthur Conan Doyle, a spiritualist who later became so weary of his most successful hero that he tried in vain to have him killed, something which even the "Hound of the Baskervilles" could not do. Some admirers still act as if Holmes not only existed but is still alive. The great private detective, had rooms in Baker Street, London. The stories are told by Dr. Watson, his faithful admirer. Holmes was always one step ahead, and explained his reading of clues to Watson, beginning "Elementary my dear Watson . . ." Holmes's genius for clue-spotting came from meticulous observation and a remarkable memory.

▼ James Bond came along when the anti-hero trend of modern life seemed a little worn. His assaults on baddies while enjoying the high life is as unrealistic as the story of Arthur. Bond, can have his cake and eat it, for he serves virtue while himself obeying no rules.

▲ Andy Capp has continued the tradition of British heroes in comic form, far from the glamour of Holmes and Arthur. Andy Capp (lazy, deceitful, materialistic, untruthful, work-shy, beer drinking) is alternately bullied and petted by his much abused wife, Flo. Andy is a hopeless case; perhaps that is why millions of Britons smile at his exploits.

Customs and superstitions

Ghosts and haunted houses

Britain has always been a country of innumerable legends, ghost stories, superstitions and ancient customs. Many traditions stretch back to pre-Christian times but are still remembered today. Even Christian festivals such as Christmas have many pagan customs incorporated into them. Mistletoe, part of the Christmas decorations in most homes, is a Druid symbol.

Clergymen still denounce black magic and dabbling in the occult which go on not only in remote areas, but even in the middle of London. Interest in spiritualism is high. Millions of people read their "stars" every day—including many who deny any belief in astrology.

Stories abound of phantom horsemen, ghostly funeral processions, haunted houses and strange noises in the night. Some clergy take such unexplained disturbances seriously enough to bless or exorcize houses affected.

The power of superstition

The increasing urbanization of Britain has, however, diluted the power of old superstitions and many ancient customs have disappeared. Though rural areas still have a rich store of old beliefs, few have been strong enough to endure transference to towns. The innumerable superstitions have been whittled down to a few, such as not walking under ladders, avoiding the unlucky number 13 or touching wood. Though their power is still strong, knowledge of their origins has been lost.

Britain has few national festivals compared with other countries. Apart from the Christian festivals of Easter and Christmas, the most popular are Hogmanay in Scotland, Guy Fawkes night, Shrove Tuesday and the National Eisteddfod in Wales. Local festivals take place throughout Britain. Some have been held continuously for hundreds of years.

The emigration of British peoples to all parts of the globe has spread many customs and superstitions world-wide. In turn Britain has absorbed customs from abroad. The Christmas tree, for instance, came to Britain from Germany.

Some British superstitions

▲ Opening an umbrella inside a house is very bad luck indeed. And unfortunately, there is no known antidote.

▲ A horseshoe is good luck, but it must be hung with the points upwards, otherwise the luck drains away.

▲ New Year's Eve is a tricky time, especially in Scotland and north England where the first across the threshold must be a dark man.

▼ Weddings still carry a full crop of superstition. The bride should wear "something old, something new, something borrowed and something blue".

▲ The fifth of November, or bonfire night, commemorates Guy Fawkes' attempt to blow up Parliament in 1605. The plot was discovered, the conspirators executed, and November 5th became a "day of national deliverance". Every year effigies of Guy Fawkes are burnt and fireworks set off to recall the explosions that never took place in Parliament.

▲ Wales has many ancient traditions which keep alive her Celtic cultural heritage. The *Eisteddfod*, a festival of music and poetry, is an occasion for dressing in traditional costumes. Each year a "bard" is chosen for his Welsh poetry.

▼ In Scotland the celebration of New Year, called *Hogmanay*, is the most important festival of the year. Traditional dress is worn by many, Scottish music played and whisky consumed in quantities.

▲ The last Tuesday before the beginning of Lent is called Shrove Tuesday and pancakes are traditionally eaten. Pancake races also take place.

The British character

▲ Standing in a queue with patience, awaiting one's fate without grumbling, is thought to be fair play.

Playing the game

What do the British think of their national character? Any Briton will believe the British to be a race of heroes after a World Cup victory, but think he belongs to a race of fools when his party loses a general election. Yet, a good deal remains of the stable notion of honour developed during the past. Strength, reliability, calmness, combined with readiness for any emergency: these qualities are believed to be in the blood. Privately, British people think they are a part of a tradition envied by others, and impossible to imitate. Britons queue for everything without trying to cut in. Newspaper stalls are left unattended in the street, in the belief that no-one would be so dishonest as to take a paper without leaving the money for it.

The Victorian tradition still remains strong, and the British think that troubles

▼ Most British people live in towns or cities, yet the pleasures of the countryside are much appreciated. Cycling and camping holidays are very popular especially among younger people.

▼ The British are devoted to their cars and frequently spend more on them than they can afford. Car grooming includes a weekly wash. Yet many cars remain standing in the road or in the garage much of the time.

and difficulties are often blessings in disguise—"to bring out the best". The ideal is to pay one's way, to know the unwritten codes of behaviour and fair play, and to be polite.

Muddling through

The British are an optimistic people. They believe that most hard times will pass; when surrounded by troubles, they plod on, preferring to avoid direct conflict, liking to see things done in the old way.

Running down Britain is a national pastime, but foreigners are never allowed to join in. There are periods of emigration, notably to Australia, but many trickle back, for Britain is cosy, and home. There is more gambling than anywhere else, for under conventional exteriors, the British are the greatest race of individuals and sheer eccentrics the world has ever seen.

▲ The British believe in remaining cool, calm and collected in every situation, no matter how hazardous.

▲ Courtesy is believed in, and sometimes practised. Few travellers actually give up their seat though everyone considers it a good thing to do.

▶ The British are gamblers. The grandest event takes place at the Ascot horse races which the Queen attends.

▲ The British are fascinated by ingenious crime. Christie, a mass-murderer, shown here has an honoured place in the Chamber of Horrors in a London waxworks.

◀ Free speech is another cherished sign of equality in public. Here a speaker at Hyde Park Corner addresses passers-by about a major British political issue—racial justice.

How Great Britain is changing

A declining prosperity?

Britain has changed dramatically since 1945. The post-war economic boom enabled living standards to be improved beyond all expectations. Today Britain is said to be facing a period of economic difficulties which will threaten future living standards. Successive governments have failed to solve the major evil—inflation. Large deposits of oil have been discovered under the North Sea. British oil should boost the economy considerably in the future. After the exhilarating experience of the last 30 years most Britons are ill-prepared for a new era of austerity.

The prosperity of Britain has caused fundamental changes in society. Increased spending power and leisure time has made life for most easier and more comfortable. Most families have a wide range of possessions from televisions to cars. Overseas holidays have come within the reach of many. Leisure activities including sport, education and gambling have increased in popularity.

Fears for the environment

The vast increase in car ownership (from 5.5 million in 1960 to 12.7 million in 1972) has given more freedom to car owners. However motor cars have changed Britain in less acceptable ways—by the sacrificing of open countryside to roads, pollution from fumes and the increase of noise. In response to such threats to the environment campaigns by both the government and citizens have been mounted to combat the excesses of an industrial society and new laws have been passed.

New freedom in society, shown in dress and habits, has dented the old class system. Women are fighting discrimination and have made some gains. Racial discrimination is another serious problem, but it is attacked, and laws exist to prevent its worst excesses. The young have gained new freedoms in all directions including expression, clothes and buying-power.

In 1973 Britain joined the European Economic Community and thus severed many links with her traditional partners in the Commonwealth. Britain is becoming increasingly aware of her changed place in the world. From being a world power, she is now becoming a European power.

▲ Oil has been found under the North Sea and off other British coasts. The discoveries could bring prosperity. providing petrol, electricity and innumerable petroleum by-products.

◄ Scottish nationalists, marching. The Scots and the Welsh have different national identities, and many nationalists believe that England has been enriched by impoverishing Scotland and Wales.

▼ Britain has a big road-building programme. There is heated debate over the wisdom of carving up the country and towns with expensive motorways.

▲ Edward Heath, Prime Minister in 1972, signing Britain into the European Economic Community. There is still disagreement as to the wisdom of this decision. The "common market" of nine countries aims at eventually achieving a common currency and possibly political federation.

▼ Large areas of Britain have been rebuilt since the war. Of all homes, 40 per cent have been built since 1944. Many offices and factories are of modern construction. Tall buildings, like these high-rise flats have been heavily criticised by many people especially the elderly and couples with young children.

▲ Nurses on strike. Strikes are traditionally a weapon of industrial workers. Recently some professional groups have gone on strike because their salaries were not keeping pace with inflation. Nurses, teachers and journalists were the first to use strike tactics.

Reference
Human and physical geography

The climate of Great Britain

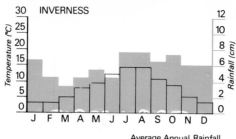
INVERNESS

Average Annual Rainfall

0-30in

30-80in

80-200in

Average Daily Sunshine

Over 5 hrs
4·5-5 hrs
4-4·5 hrs
3·5-4 hrs
3-3·5
Under 3hrs

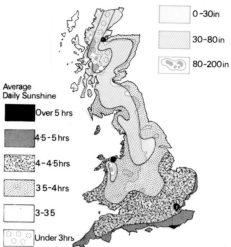

Climate
Britain has a temperate and mild climate. The prevailing winds are from the south-west. Winds are generally stronger in the north than in the south of the British Isles and stronger on the coasts than inland. The weather is liable to frequent changes but to few extremes of temperature (the average range between summer and winter is from 7°C to 12°C).

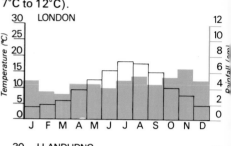
LONDON

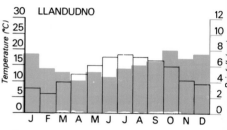
LLANDUDNO

The natural vegetation of Great Britain

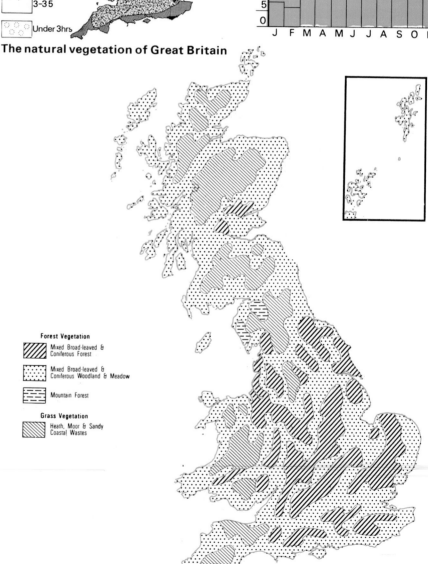

Forest Vegetation
- Mixed Broad-leaved & Coniferous Forest
- Mixed Broad-leaved & Coniferous Woodland & Meadow
- Mountain Forest

Grass Vegetation
- Heath, Moor & Sandy Coastal Wastes

The population density

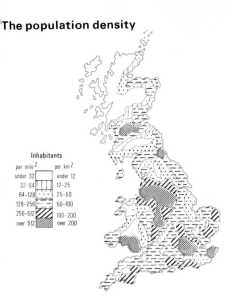

Inhabitants

per mile²	per km²
under 32	under 12
32–64	12–25
64–128	25–50
128–256	50–100
256–512	100–200
over 512	over 200

In mid 1972 the estimated population of Great Britain was 54,239,000. In 1700 it was 6.5 million and in 1901 38.2 million. A great reduction in death rates, and high birth rates were the main causes of this great increase. Present trends indicate that the increase is likely to continue, reaching 57.3 million people in 1981, 59.8 million in 1991 and 62.4 million in 2001.

Migration has been important to Britain. Between 1871 and 1931 four million more people left the country than came into it. Since 1931 Britain has seen more immigration than emigration. In 1960-2 total net immigration was 388,000 people, mainly from the Commonwealth. Immigration controls have now stemmed this flow considerably.

Population of principal towns

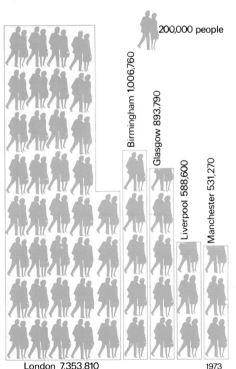

200,000 people

Birmingham 1,006,760
Glasgow 893,790
Liverpool 588,600
Manchester 531,270
London 7,353,810
1973

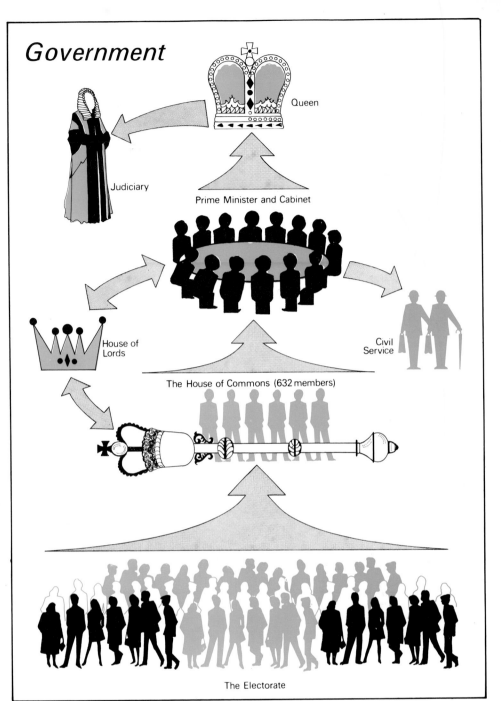

Government

Queen

Judiciary

Prime Minister and Cabinet

House of Lords

Civil Service

The House of Commons (632 members)

The Electorate

The unwritten constitution
The British system of government has evolved through many hundreds of years and has been changed constantly to meet changing requirements. The sovereign once had complete power but now is said to ''reign but not rule''. The United Kingdom of Great Britain and Northern Ireland is governed by Her Majesty's Government *in the name of the Queen.* The Queen acts only on the advice of her ministers.

The two Houses
The British Parliament consists of two parts — the House of Lords and the elected House of Commons. Both Houses have the same functions, i.e. to pass laws, to make finance available and to put important

issues before the electorate. However the power of the Lords has been drastically reduced and the Commons is the real seat of parliamentary power. The Commons is elected by almost all citizens over 18 years.

The Government
The political party which has the most Members of the House of Commons elected in a general election, forms the Government. The leader of this party becomes the Prime Minister and he chooses the members of his government. The most important ministers in the government form the Cabinet which makes government policy. The Cabinet must however have the support of its party both in Parliament and more generally in the country itself.

Main Events in British History

B.C.

700-300	Celtic invasions from Europe bring iron to Britain.
55	Julius Caesar invades Britain.

A.D.

5-50	Roman Conquest of Britain.
48-79	Conquest of Wales.
410-22	Romans leave Britain. Invasion of Angles, Saxons and Jutes begins.
664	Roman Church becomes supreme in England by Synod of Whitby.
856-75	Viking invasion.
871-99	Alfred the Great resists Vikings but cannot prevent conquest of large area.
899	Alfred's son Edward reclaims land lost to Vikings. First true English king.
1066	Norman invasion. William the Conqueror defeats Harold at Battle of Hastings.
1106	Conquest of Normandy by Henry I.
1170	British opposition to Roman Church shown by assassination of Thomas à Becket.
1215	Barons force King John to sign Magna Carta which upholds their rights.
1283	Edward I conquers Wales.
1314	Scotland ensures independence at Battle of Bannockburn.
1337	Edward III claims French throne and thus begins Hundred Years' War.
1415	Henry V defeats French at Battle of Agincourt.
1455-85	Wars of Roses: Houses of York and Lancaster fight for throne.
1485	Henry Tudor defeats Richard III at Battle of Bosworth Field and becomes Henry VII.
1487	Court of Star Chamber puts judiciary under king.
1534	Henry VIII abolishes Papal authority in England and establishes Church of England.
1553-8	Mary Tudor brings back Roman Catholic Church.
1558	England loses Calais, last hold in France. Mary Queen of Scots deposed.
1559	Elizabeth I makes English Church supreme again.
1587	Mary Queen of Scots executed.
1588	Spanish Armada defeated.
1603	James VI of Scotland also becomes James I of England. Crowns united.
1605	Gunpowder Plot fails.
1641	"Long Parliament" tries to limit royal power but Charles I objects.
1642-8	Civil War between "Roundheads" (Puritans) and "Cavaliers" (Royalists).
1649	Cromwell sets up Commonwealth. Charles I beheaded.
1653-8	Protectorate with Cromwell as Lord Protector.
1660	Restoration of monarchy — Charles II.
1688	James II deposed. William and Mary offered crown.
1692	Scottish rebels massacred at Glencoe.
1707	Act of Union creates Great Britain.
1715	Jacobite rebellion against George I defeated.
1756	Seven Years War with France begins.
1757	Clive wins French land in India.
1759	Wolfe wins Battle of Quebec and gains Canada.
1775-83	American War of Independence.
1793-1815	Wars against French revolutionaries and Napoleon. Final victory at Waterloo 1815.
1807	Slave trade abolished.
1825	Stockton to Darlington railway opened.
1832	Trade unions founded. Reform Bill widens electorate.
1833	Factory Act sets nine as minimum working age.
1839-42	Opium War with China.
1854-6	Crimean War against Russia.
1859	Darwin's *Origin of Species* published.
1875	Suez Canal comes under British control.
1899-1902	Boer War gives Britain control of Transvaal and Orange Free State.
1900	British Labour Party founded.
1905-14	Period of liberal reform.
1910	Union of South Africa created.
1914-18	World War I against Germany.
1922	Irish Free State formed.
1926	General Strike.
1930	Great depression. Great unemployment.
1936	Abdication of Edward VIII.
1939	War declared with Germany September 3.
1940	Battle of Britain.
1944	Allied landings in Normandy June 6.
1945	Germany and Japan surrender.
1945-51	Labour Party creates Welfare State.
1947	Partition of India.
1951	Conservatives under Churchill regain power.
1956	Invasion of Suez. Britain loses control of Canal.
1959	Many colonies given independence.
1964	Labour Party, under Harold Wilson, wins election.
1968-	Hostility between Protestants and Catholics in Northern Ireland develops into near-civil war.
1970	Conservative Party, under Edward Heath, regains power. First major oil discoveries in North Sea.
1973	Britain joins European Economic Community.
1974	Labour wins election with small majority.

Kings and Queens of England

Saxons and Danes

802-39	Egbert
839-58	Ethelwulf
858-60	Ethelbald
860-6	Ethelbert
866-71	Ethelred
871-99	Alfred the Great
899-924	Edward the Elder
924-40	Aethelstan
940-6	Edmund
946-55	Edred
955-9	Edwy
959-75	Edgar
975-8	Edward the Martyr
978-1016	Ethelred the Unready
1016	Edmund Ironside
1016-35	Canute the Dane
1035-40	Harold I
1040-2	Harthacnut
1042-66	Edward the Confessor
1066	Harold II

House of Normandy

1066-87	William I (the Conqueror)
1087-1100	William II
1100-35	Henry I
1135-54	Stephen

House of Plantagenet

1154-89	Henry II
1189-99	Richard I (Lionheart)
1199-1216	John
1216-72	Henry III
1272-1307	Edward I
1307-27	Edward II
1327-77	Edward III
1377-99	Richard II

House of Lancaster

1399-1413	Henry IV
1413-22	Henry V
1422-61	Henry VI

House of York

1461-83	Edward IV
1483	Edward V
1483-5	Richard III

House of Tudor

1485-1509	Henry VII
1509-47	Henry VIII
1547-53	Edward VI
1553-8	Mary Tudor (Mary I)
1558-1603	Elizabeth I

House of Stuart

1603-25	James I
1625-49	Charles I

[1649-60 **Commonwealth** (No king)]

1660-85	Charles II
1685-8	James II
1689-94	William III and Mary II
1694-1702	William III
1702-14	Anne

House of Hanover

1714-27	George I
1727-60	George II

The Arts

LITERATURE

Geoffrey Chaucer (c. 1340-1400) poet and chronicler *Canterbury Tales*
William Shakespeare (1564-1616) greatest English dramatist and poet
John Donne (1572-1631) poet and sermon writer
John Milton (1608-74) poet of *Paradise Lost, L'Allegro, Il Penseroso,* etc.
John Dryden (1631-1700) poet and playwright *All for Love*
Samuel Pepys (1633-1703) the celebrated diarist
Daniel Defoe (1660-1731) author *Robinson Crusoe, Moll Flanders, Diary of the Plague*
Jonathan Swift (1667-1745) *Gulliver's Travels, A Tale of a Tub,* other satires
Alexander Pope (1688-1744) poet *Essay on Man*
Dr. Samuel Johnson (1709-84) poet, essayist, critic. Compiled the first English dictionary
Laurence Sterne (1713-68) *The Life and Opinions of Tristram Shandy*
Oliver Goldsmith (c. 1730-74) *The Vicar of Wakefield, She Stoops to Conquer*
Richard Brinsley Sheridan (1751-1816) *School for Scandal, The Rivals, The Critic*
William Blake (1757-1827) poet, philosopher and visionary painter
Robert Burns (1759-96) Scottish national poet
William Wordsworth (1770-1850) poet and critic *The Excursion,* sonnets, play *The Borderers*
Sir Walter Scott (1771-1832) *Ivanhoe,* the Waverley novels, *The Lady of the Lake*
Jane Austen (1775-1817) novelist *Price and Prejudice, Emma, Persuasion*
Lord Byron (1788-1824) *Don Juan, Childe Harold's Pilgrimage, Prisoner of Chillon*
Percy Bysshe Shelley (1792-1822) poet *To a Skylark, Ode to the West Wind*
John Keats (1795-1821) poems, sonnets, odes *Endymion, Eve of St. Agnes, Hyperion*
Lord Alfred Tennyson (1809-92) poet, *The Princess*
Charles Dickens (1812-1870) *David Copperfield, Great Expectations, Little Dorrit*
Robert Browning (1812-89) poet and playwright *The Ring and the Book, Pippa Passes*
Charlotte Brönte (1816-55) poet and novelist *Jane Eyre, Villette*
Emily Brönte (1816-48) poet and novelist *Wuthering Heights*
Mary Ann Evans (George Eliot) (1819-80) novelist *Adam Bede, Middlemarch, The Mill on the Floss*
Thomas Hardy (1840-1928) poet and novelist *The Mayor of Casterbridge, Tess of the D'Urbervilles*
Oscar Wilde (1854-1900) *The Importance of Being Ernest,* other plays, poems
George Bernard Shaw (1856-1950) playwright *Pygmalion, St. Joan, Candida*

H. G. Wells (1866-1946) *Outline of History, War of the Worlds, The Time Machine*
Bertrand Russell (1872-1970) *Philosophy and Politics,* various essays
Somerset Maugham (1874-1965) *Of Human Bondage, Razor's Edge,* short stories
Virginia Woolf (1882-1941) novelist and critic *The Years, Mrs. Dalloway*
D. H. Lawrence (1885-1930) poet and novelist *Sons and Lovers, Women in Love*
Aldous Huxley (1894-19) essayist, novelist, poet
W. H. Auden (1907-1973) poet of *The Age of Anxiety, The Double Man*
Dylan Thomas (1914-53) poet *Under Milk Wood, Adventures in the Skin Trade*

MUSIC

Henry Purcell (1658-95) operas *Dido and Aeneas,* theatre and other music
George Frederick Handel (1685-1759) *Messiah,* many operas
Sir Arthur Sullivan (1842-1900) operettas with W. S. Gilbert, *Lost Chord*
Sir Edward Elgar (1857-1934) *Enigma Variations, Dream of Gerontius,* symphonies
Frederick Delius (1862-1934) *Mass of Life,* opera *Village Romeo and Juliet*
Ralph Vaughan Williams (1872-1958) *A London Symphony,* operas, chamber music
Sir William Walton (1902-19) *Facade* symphonies, film music
Benjamin Britten (1913-19) *War Requiem* operas *Peter Grimes, Billy Budd*

VISUAL ARTS/ARCHITECTURE

Inigo Jones (1573-1652) Palladian architect
Sir Christopher Wren (1632-1723) architect of St. Paul's Cathedral and 51 London churches
William Hogarth (1697-1764) Satirist of *A Rake's Progress,* artist/engraver
Sir Joshua Reynolds (1723-92) Portrait painter and experimentor
Robert Adam (1728-92) innovator interior design, furniture, decoration
Thomas Gainsborough (1727-88) landscape and portrait artist *The Blue Boy*
George Romney (1734-1802) fashionable portraits
Joseph M. W. Turner (1775-1851) landscape artist, semi-abstract innovator/experimentor
John Constable (1776-1837) landscapes pre-impressionist originality of light/motion
William Morris (1834-96) founder co-op arts and crafts, painter/decorator
Augustus John (1879-1961) painter of portraits
Sir Jacob Epstein (1880-1959) sculptor
Henry Moore (1898-19) sculptor, drawings of blitz
Graham Sutherland (1903-) portraits, landscapes
Francis Bacon (1909-) figures
Brigit Riley (1931-) dimensional patterns

FACTS AND FIGURES

The economy

Gross National Product:
£53,940 m. (1972).

Economic Growth Rate: 2.4% per year (1965-70).

Main sources of income:

Agriculture: wheat, barley, oats, potatoes, sugar beet, cattle, sheep, lambs, pigs, poultry, dairy products, vegetables, fruit, flowers.

Fishing: cod, haddock, plaice, whiting, sole, skate, herring, shellfish.

Mining: coal, limestone, iron ore, sandstone, salt, china clay, fireclay, chalk, gypsum, oil shale, lead ore, tin ore, and silicon. Large deposits of oil and gas in North Sea.

Industry: machinery, chemicals, woollen and synthetic textiles, motor vehicles, iron and steel, locomotives, aircraft, farm machinery, drugs, electrical equipment, whisky.

Main trading partners: United States, West Germany, France, the Commonwealth.

Currency: £1 = 100 new pence. Exchange rates vary. £1 = $2.35 (January 1975)

Budget: Expenditure (1972-3) £27,884 million (Defence £3,003 million, Education £3,569 million, Social Security £5,050 million).

Economy

The current state of the British economy causes concern. Prophets of doom out-number the consoling optimism of whatever government is in power. The main worries are inflation, (as everywhere else) and deficits in the balance of payments situation. Britain tends to import more than is exported. Other major ills are shortage of investment capital, and a sluggish increase in production. Much is made of labour unrest, with blame cast on the unions. However statistics do not put Britain at the top of world tables in time lost by strikes. One of the trickiest problems facing any British government is the fine line between encouraging consumer spending, and controlling credit. The spectre of nationwide unemployment, with over a million people out of work, haunts the British economy. Membership of the European Common Market is too recent to evaluate fully but it should give Britain vast new markets if the problems of industry can be solved. North Sea oil discoveries give further hope that Britain will be able to improve the economy.

Agriculture in Great Britain

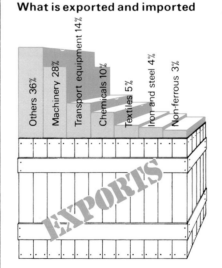

What is exported and imported

In the 19th century British trade dominated the world. Today more powerful nations have come to the fore, though Britain still ranks fourth in world trade.

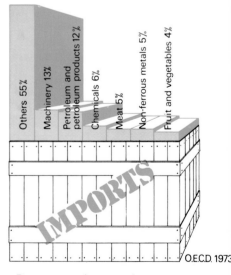

O.E.C.D. 1973

Recent years however have seen a decline in the British ability to compete with other countries. Because of her dependence on world trade the British standard of living is threatened.

How labour is employed

Total population 55,930,000

Wealth produced

Non-working population 31,221,000

Military 2%

Industry 46.6%

Others 48.5%

Agriculture 2.9%

Britain has fewer people engaged in agriculture than other major industrial countries. A high level of productivity enables agriculture to supply over half of the food needed. The proportion of workers in industry has remained constant for several years. Transport, communications, health and educational services have however increased their share of both workers and output.

Industry in Great Britain

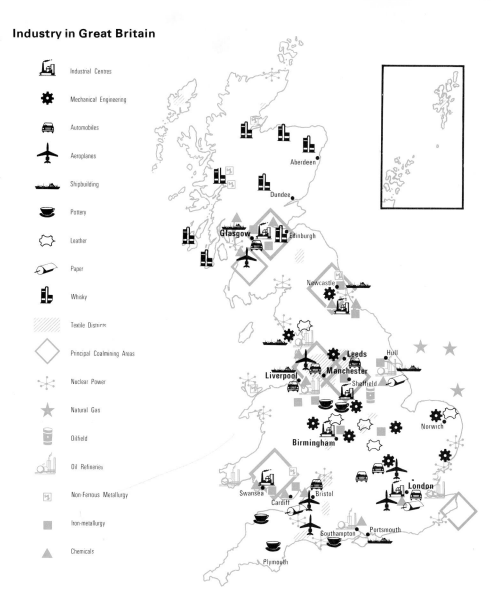

🏭	Industrial Centres	
⚙	Mechanical Engineering	
🚗	Automobiles	
✈	Aeroplanes	
🚢	Shipbuilding	
☕	Pottery	
	Leather	
	Paper	
	Whisky	
▨	Textile Districts	
◇	Principal Coalmining Areas	
☀	Nuclear Power	
★	Natural Gas	
	Oilfield	
	Oil Refineries	
M	Non-Ferrous Metallurgy	
▪	Iron-metallurgy	
▲	Chemicals	

Aberdeen
Dundee
Glasgow
Edinburgh
Newcastle
Leeds
Hull
Liverpool
Manchester
Sheffield
Norwich
Birmingham
Swansea
Cardiff
Bristol
London
Southampton
Portsmouth
Plymouth

What is owned compared with other countries

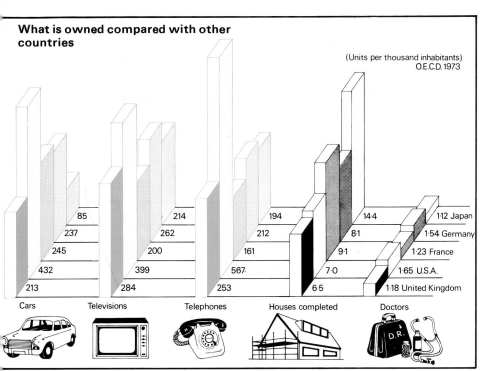

(Units per thousand inhabitants)
O.E.C.D. 1973

	Cars	Televisions	Telephones	Houses completed	Doctors	
	85	214	194	14.4	1.12	Japan
	237	262	212	8.1	1.54	Germany
	245	200	161	9.1	1.23	France
	432	399	567	7.0	1.65	U.S.A.
	213	284	253	6.5	1.18	United Kingdom

Cars   Televisions   Telephones   Houses completed   Doctors

The rise in prices and wages

(Percentage increase)

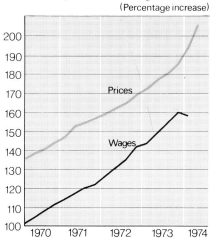

Prices

Wages

1970 1971 1972 1973 1974

The most serious problem facing Britain at present is inflation (rise in prices). Prices of imported goods have risen sharply. Wage demands have increased to keep pace but with inflation predicted to be 20%+ for years to come, the British standard of living is threatened.

Gazetteer

Birmingham (52 29N 1 54W) England. Second largest British city. Grew greatly during the Industrial Revolution from a market town. Estimated 1500 trades carried on. Pop. (1972) 1,008,000.

Bradford (53 48N 1 46W) England. Centre for woollen and other textile manufacture. Many other industries. Pop. (1971) 293,756.

Bristol (51 28N 2 36W) England. Seaport and industrial centre. Settled in late Saxon times, developed through wool and slave trades to Americas. Pop. (1972) 421,580.

Cambridge (52 11N 0 8E) England. Famous university town. First college, Peterhouse, founded in 1289. Important in middle ages as a route centre and port. Tourist centre. Pop. (1972) 98,840.

Canterbury (51 15N 1 6E) England. Cathedral city and headquarters of the English Church. Magnificent Cathedral with great mixture of architectural styles. Pop. (1972) 36,290.

Cardiff (51 29N 3 10W) Capital of Wales. Seaport. Administrative centre. Manufactures aircraft, chocolate, soap, tobacco products. Developed rapidly in 19th C. with development of S. Wales coal and iron fields. Pop. (1972) 274,920.

Clyde (55 38N 3 47W) Most important Scottish river. Major industrial towns e.g. Lanark, Hamilton, Glasgow, Clydebank, and Dumbarton are on its banks.

Coventry (52 25N 1 31W) England. Industrial centre. Manufactures cars, bicycles, machinery, electrical equipment, hosiery. Controversial modern cathedral. Pop. (1972) 336,370.

Dundee (56 27N 2 58W) Scotland. Seaport. Centre of British jute industry. Pop. (1972) 182,930.

Edinburgh (55 57N 3 12W) Capital of Scotland. Business, cultural and administrative centre. Dominated by ancient castle where international festival is held every year. Main occupations, printing, publishing, whisky distilling, confectionery, chemicals. Pop. (1972) 543,025.

Forth (56 8N 4 15W) Scottish river, 106km long. Crossed by several bridges and has on its banks, Stirling, ports of Leith, Grangemouth and the Naval base at Rosyth.

Glasgow (55 52N 4 14W) Largest city in Scotland. Seaport and industrial centre. Growth largely due to position on R. Clyde as can be reached by ocean-going vessels. Main industries, ship-building, engineering, flour milling, textiles, chemicals, distillery, soap, clothing, food products. Pop. (1971) 893,790.

Grampians (56 42N 4 27W) Scottish mountain range between Glenmore and Central Lowlands. Includes Ben Nevis (highest point in G.B., 1341m.).

Hebrides (57 40N 7 0W) Scotland. Group of about 500 islands off W. coast. About 100 inhabited. Comprised of Inner and Outer Hebrides.

Inverness (57 28N 4 12W) Scotland. County town, commercial and tourist centre. Seaport. Often called the "Capital of the Highlands". Pop. (1972) 34,426.

Kingston-Upon-Hull (53 45N 0 20W) England. Seaport for export of goods from N. and Midlands. Biggest fishing port in Britain. Large manufacturing industry. Pop. (1962) 282,870.

Lake District (54 28N 3 13W) England. Region of lakes and mountains. Includes highest point in England, Scafell Pikes (978m.).

Leeds (53 49N 1 33W) England. Industrial centre. Main products, ready-made clothing, diesel engines, textile and printing machinery, agricultural and electrical equipment, furniture, chemicals. Pop. (1972) 498,790.

Leicester (52 37N 1 6W) England. Industrial centre. Manufactures hosiery, footwear, textiles. Engineering. Pop. (1972) 281,440.

Liverpool (53 25N 3 0W) England. Second most important sea-port in Britain and major industrial centre. Founded by Norsemen but grew rapidly with American trade in 18th and 19th centuries. Badly damaged in World War II. Industries include electrical engineering, sugar refining, chemicals, flour milling. Pop. (1972) 588,600.

London (51 30N 0 5W) Capital of England and United Kingdom. Chief seaport, financial, commercial, industrial, cultural and governmental administrative centre. Route centre. Developed by Romans in first century A.D. Today Greater London covers an area of 620 sq. miles and is divided into 32 boroughs. Pop. (1971) 7,400,000.

Man, Isle of (54 10N 4 35W) Island in the Irish Sea. Has own Parliament, the Court of Tynwald, and is not bound by Acts of the British Parliament unless specifically mentioned in them. Capital, Douglas. Agriculture, cattle and tourism.

Manchester (53 28N 2 15W) England. Great commercial centre and inland port. Principally concerned with cotton industry, textile machinery. The Manchester Ship Canal (built 1887-94) connects it with the sea. Grew during the Industrial Revolution but founded as *Mancunium* during Roman times. Pop. (1972) 531,270.

Nottingham (52 58N 1 8W) England. Important industrial centre involved in hosiery, bicycles, cigarettes, pharmaceuticals, brewing, engineering. Pop. (1972) 295,000.

Orkney Islands (59 3N 3 0W) Scotland. Group of about 70 islands. Mostly low-lying and bleak. Under Norse rule until 1468.

Oxford (51 45N 1 15W) England. Famous university town. First college founded in 13th C. but mentioned in 10th C. as educational centre. Much splendid architecture. Today has also become an industrial centre, especially for car-making. Route centre.

Pennine Chain (54 20N 2 10W) England. System of hills, sometimes known as "the backbone of England".

Plymouth (50 22N 4 10W) England. Important naval base, seaport and industrial centre. In Elizabethan times it was the country's chief port. Pop. (1972) 252,000.

Portsmouth (50 47N 1 7W) England. Chief naval base. Nicknamed "Pompey". Became important during reign of Henry VIII. Seriously damaged in World War II. Birthplace of Charles Dickens. Pop. (1972) 207,000.

Severn, River (51 40N 2 35W) England. 337km. long. Has many important tributaries and large estuary entering into Bristol Channel. Famous also for its high tidal bore.

Scilly Isles (49 55N 6 20W) England. Group of about 140 islands off the coast of Cornwall. Mild climate enables early crops to be grown. Tourism centre.

Sheffield (52 23N 1 28W) England. Leading iron and steel centre. By 14th C. it was famous for its cutlery and grew rapidly during the Industrial Revolution. Pop. (1972) 515,000.

Shetland Islands (60 20N 1 20W) Scotland. Archipelago of over 100 islands. Largely barren.

Snowdon (53 4N 4 10W) Wales. Highest mountain in England and Wales, (1,683m.). The Snowdonia National Park is a popular tourist area.

Southampton (50 55N 1 24W) England. Chief British passenger seaport. Also handles large volume of imports and exports. Large oil refinery at Fawley, south of city. Pop. (1972) 214,000.

Stirling (56 7N 3 55W) Scotland. Ancient town known as "gateway to the Highlands". Dominated by castle where Mary Queen of Scots and James IV were crowned.

Stoke-on-Trent (53 2N 2 12W) England. Centre of pottery industry. Wedgwood, Spode, and Minton China made here. Pop. (1972) 263,000.

Stratford-upon-Avon (52 11N 1 43W) England. Celebrated as birthplace of Shakespeare (1564-1616) and because of this has become an important centre for tourism.

Swansea (51 38N 3 57W) Wales. Sea port and industrial centre. Centre for tin-plate manufacture. Pop (1972) 171,520.

Thames, River (51 52N 0 47W) England. Chief river, 337km. long, beginning in the Cotswold Hills and flowing through many important towns including London. Great economic importance as enormous amount of trade passes through the Port of London.

Winchester (51 4N 1 19W) England. Ancient Cathedral city. Route centre, and market town. Founded in Roman times and rivalled London as a royal centre in the Middle Ages. Pop. (1972) 31,620.

York (53 58N 1 5W) England. Important commercial, industrial and route centre. As *Eboracum* it was military capital of Roman Britain. Its Archbishop ranks second only to the Archbishop of Canterbury. Famous cathedral (begun 1154) known as York Minster, has world famous stained glass. Pop. (1972) 104,780.

Index

Numbers in **heavy** type refer to illustrations

3 4 5 6 7 8 9 10-McN-81 80 79 78